I am Kind.

I am Strong.

I choose to be Healthy.

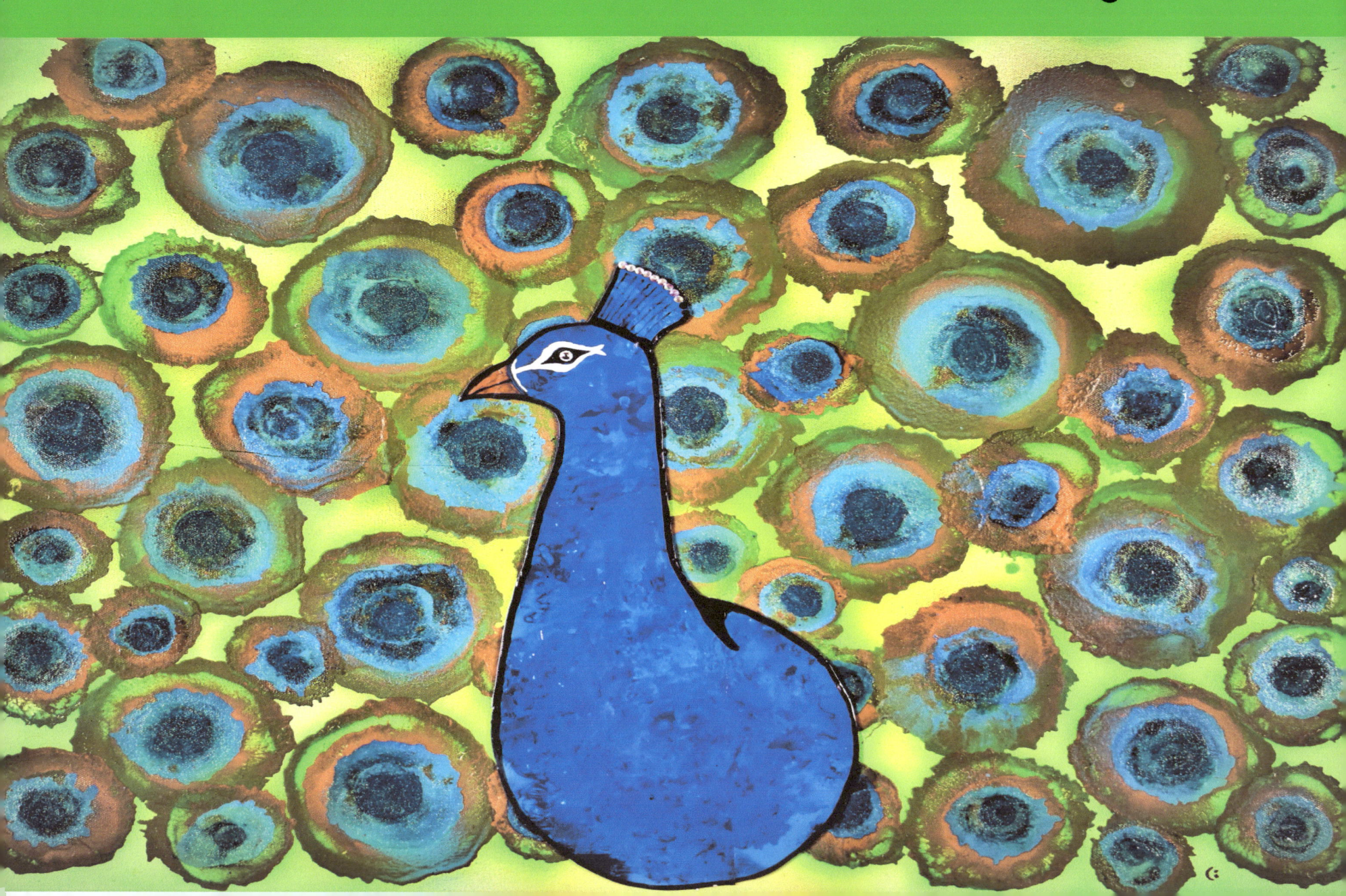

I am Amazing.

I make friends easily.

I am Talented.

I can think of many things.

I am Bold.

I love to Play.

I am stronger than I appear.

I am Helpful.

I choose to grow Big and Strong.

I can see Good everywhere.

I can
be
Calm.

I can be Quiet.

I see Beauty all around me.

I am a Miracle.

I will choose good things for My Self.

LOVE. FAITH. FORGIVENESS. FAITH. HEALING. CONFIDENCE. STRENGTH. PEACE. INSPIRATION. GRATITUDE. CALM.

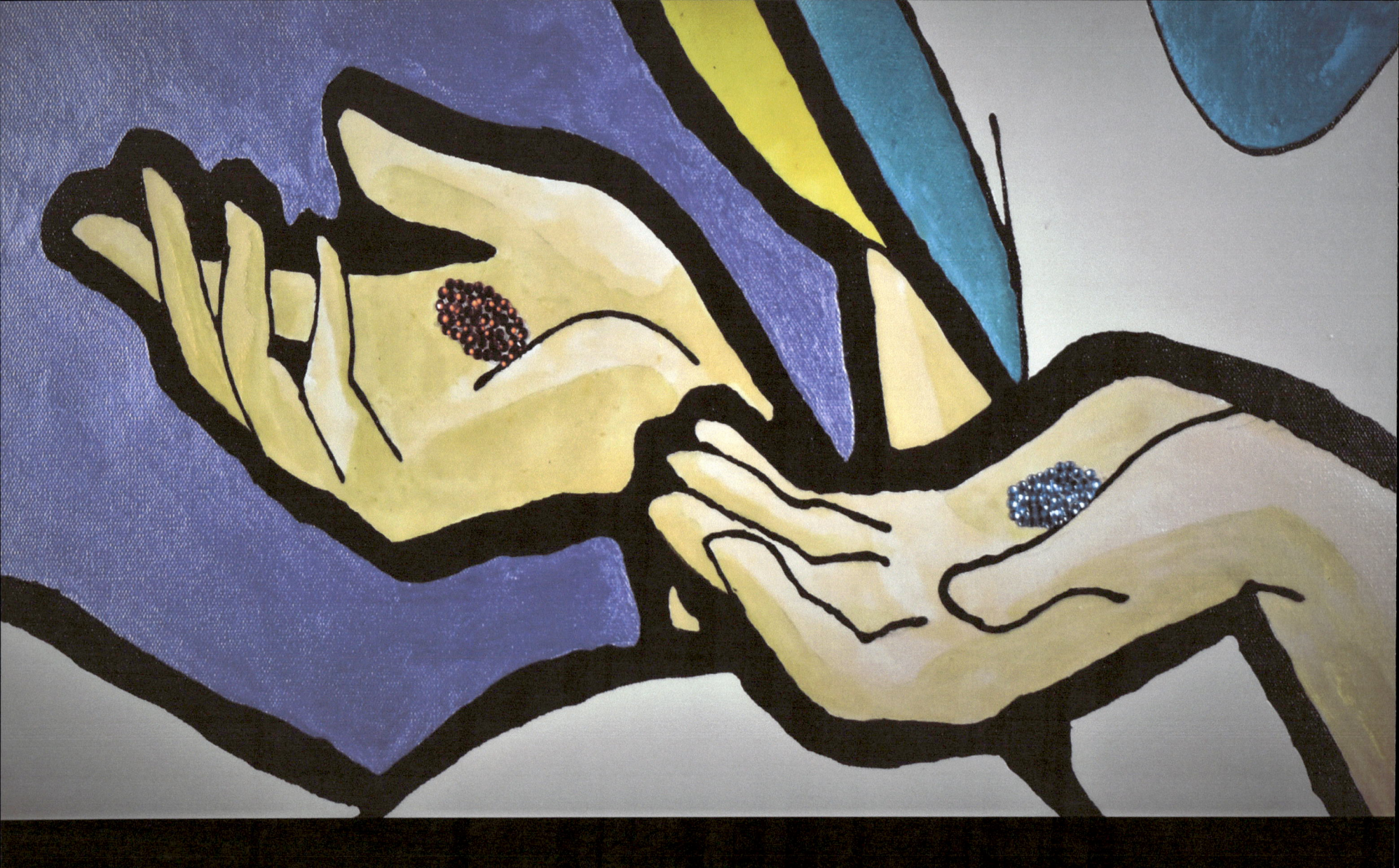

I am Thankful, Grateful, Relaxed, And Blessed.

I like to play outside.

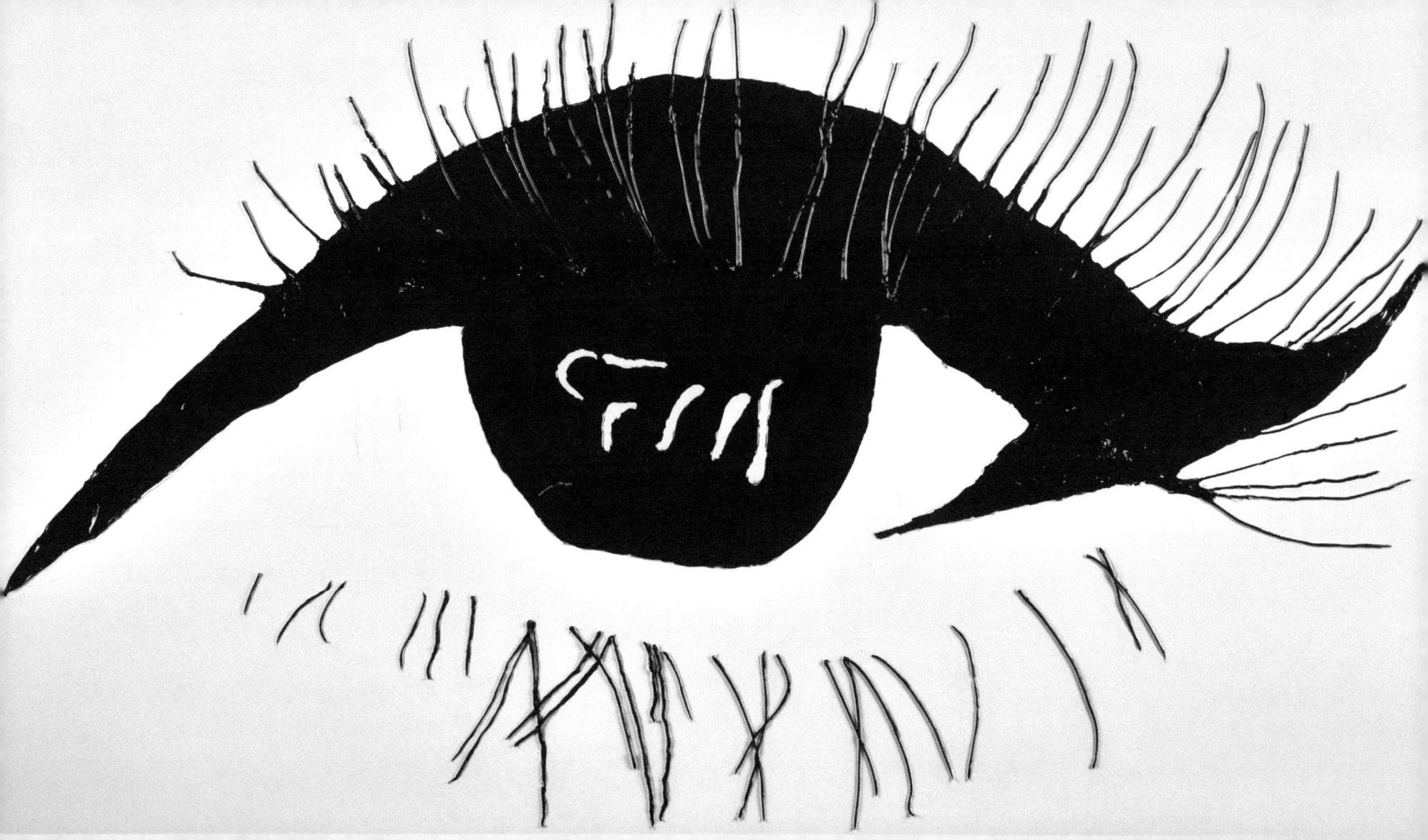

I choose
the way I think.

I am more than enough.
I am more than enough.
I am more than enough.
I am more than enough.

Thank you.

Dee McClure - Jo Ann Jonas - Debra Benton

Tina, Maria, Jerry, Rosa, Kurt, Francie, Sergio, Miguel, Hilda, Avel, Michele, Angelina, Veronika, Marisela, Adriana, Seamus, Mikey, Athena, Daphne, Luna, Michael, Loreen, Jerry, Kyle, Randy, Dennis, Cindy, Marnell, Jimmy, Norma, Ally, Dan, Tracy, Karen, Rick, Debby, Chris, Mick, Sean, Kurt, Antoinette, Don, Anne, Lane, Doris, Larry, Jamie, Kevin, Connie, Doug, Rick, Kathy, Evelyn, Tammy, Barbara, Yolanda, Kevin, Stacy, Angelica, Pam, Kathee, Miles, Lauren, and Jesus.

THANK YOU TO ALL THAT PREVIEWED THIS BOOK AT EL CHARRO AVITIA

A special thank you to my hometown Bishop, CA

Art encourages us to imagine and anticipate
a better Self, community, and world.   Tony Avitia

Copyright © 2018 by Tony Avitia

All rights reserved. No part of this publication may be reproduced, distributed, or transmitted in any form or by any means, including photocopying, recording, or other electronic or mechanical methods, without the prior written permission of the publisher, except in the case of brief quotations embodied in critical reviews and certain other noncommercial uses permitted by copyright law. For permission requests, write to Amuzed Art at amuzedart@yahoo.com

Amuzed Art LLC.
4389 S. Carson St.
Carson City, NV. 89701

amuzedart@yahoo.com   www.selfregards.com   amuzedart.com

ISBN 9780999697825   Library of Congress Control Number: 2018900463

www.ingramcontent.com/pod-product-compliance
Lightning Source LLC
Chambersburg PA
CBHW050855010526
44118CB00004BA/170